# A HISTORY OF
# SYSTEMOLOGY

## POCKET EDITION

Published from
Mardukite Borsippa HQ, San Luis Valley, Colorado
Mardukite Academy & Systemology Society
*for spiritual or educational purposes only*

# A HISTORY OF SYSTEMOLOGY

## EVOLUTION OF A SPIRITUAL SCIENCE

A Basic Course developed
by Joshua Free
for the Systemology Society

© 2023, JOSHUA FREE

ISBN : 978-1-961509-22-1

*Also available in hardcover as*
*"Fundamentals of Systemology"*

Pocket Paperback Edition — *October 2023*

**mardukite.com**

**SYSTEMOLOGY is the
"New Thought" of the 21st Century.**

It is the study of how
Spiritual Beings with unlimited power
became entrapped in the
Human Condition.

This study is an applied philosophy
— "A Pathway to Ascension" —
that charts our way back out,
freeing the True Self to experience
higher levels of existence again.

Systemology is the true science of the
"Matrix."

After more than a decade of
development, the "Fundamentals of
Systemology" are concisely explored
here in the first official
"Basic Course" on the subject ever
given by Joshua Free for the
Mardukite Academy.

It's time to discover
who you really are...
because you
were never "Human."

Fundamentals of Systemology
Basic Course Lesson Booklets

*Lesson #1*
BEING MORE THAN HUMAN
Rediscovering the Spiritual Self

*Lesson #2*
REALITIES IN AGREEMENT
Spiritual Life and The Universe

*Lesson #3*
WINDOWS TO EXPERIENCE
The Filters of Human Perception

*Lesson #4*
ANCIENT SYSTEMOLOGY
Wisdom From the Arcane Tablets

*Lesson #5*
A HISTORY OF SYSTEMOLOGY
Evolution of a Spiritual Science

*Lesson #6*
SYSTEMOLOGY PROCESSING
Practices of Spiritual Awakening

# TABLET OF CONTENTS

# INTRODUCTION
# TO THE
# "BASIC COURSE"

## WELCOME, SEEKER!
## YOUR JOURNEY ON THE PATHWAY
## BEGINS HERE

This is a basic course in *Systemology*—specifically, the fundamental principles of *Mardukite Systemology.*

Quite simply: *Mardukite Systemology* is a new evolution in Human understanding about the "systems" governing *Spiritual Life*, *Reality*, the *Universe* and all *Existences*.

In many ways, *Systemology* is a 21st Century breakthrough that continues the legacy—and unifies the original pursuits—of early 20th Century *"American New Thought"* and other metaphysical schools of philosophy and mysticism. These are mostly all generalized (and often dismissed) in modern culture as *"New Age"* beliefs, though they are actually quite *"old"* —some even based on the most ancient known writings of discovered civilizations.

*Mardukite Systemology* was once concisely described as "an applied spiritual technology of the 21st Century A.D., based on spiritual wisdom from the 21st Century B.C." because of our use of *"Mesopotamian" Arcane Tablets* as source material for its foundations (and from which it retains a *"Mardukite"* designation).

The original *New Thought Movement* in America applied a "Western Civilization" approach to "Eastern" concepts—concepts that we now take for granted today, but of which were relatively unknown to the general population at that time. The movement sought to develop an "applied spiritual philosophy" whereby an individual could unlock their hidden potentials, untapped *"Knowingness"* and higher spiritual states of *Beingness*. These innate or native conditions of *Self* (as a *Spirit*) are blocked—or "fragmented"—by a "human" preoccupation with identifying *Self* as one and the same with the material body that it is merely using as a "vehicle" to experience (communicate and interact) within *this* Physical Universe.

Early *New Thought* work primarily emphasized practical "healing" applications (*mental healing, faith healing, &tc.*)—but at its very core, we may restate the ultimate pursuit or original focus was to "free humans *to be* their ideal native spiritual state."

This goal has been with us—lingering on the periphery of the "surface world"—for much longer than the existence of a *New Thought Movement*. In fact, for as long as "spiritual beings" have found themselves entrapped by a "Human Condition" and enforced to experience *this* "material existence" (fragmented from their true *Self*), a continuing pursuit has ensued to correct the situation—at least by those individuals still retaining enough *Awareness* to realize it.

Humans have been figuring on how to break free from the *"Matrix"* for a very long time. The desire or ambition to rise above the "standard-issue" Human Condition is already there. But the truth is that many other remotely similar "evolutions" of *New Thought* have dissolved into "multi-level marketing" schemes, "motivational pop-psychology" coaching, abusive "cult-like" movements—or heavily promoted books that skyrocket to the peaks of literary "bestseller lists" only to be discarded soon after and forgotten. They all share one thing in common: they all seem to capitalize on an innate desire or yearning we have to *"ascend"*—but, of course, without delivering stable results.

Even the most pious and well-meaning

philosophies and spiritual sciences have each fallen short of piercing the *"invisible barriers"* of perception separating *this* "Physical Universe" from any other "higher" existence—and with it, blocking our "way out" and the *Awareness* of our own true native state as an *Eternal Spirit*.

---

## SYSTEMOLOGY:
## 21ST CENTURY NEW THOUGHT

Our *Systemology* is a new approach to *"Self-Actualization"*—completely relevant for the modern age and the future—and quite different from previous attempts or other traditions you might find.

Former attempts at overcoming *"barriers"* or *"gates"* of *reality* have included simply pretending that they don't exist, rejecting all material existence—all *time* and *space* —as an *"illusion"* and consequently losing the ability to actually *confront* the *reality* of anything *"As-It-Is."*

Our *Systemology* is also the answer to the "great mysteries" pervading the material sciences and natural philosophies; for they only seek to further qualify and validate the *reality agreements* made for *this* Physical Universe—and thus their level of understanding can never successfully pass the "barriers" either.

When applying our philosophy and techniques, the "systematic routes" outlined for an individual to increase their *"Actualized Awareness"* (and reach gradually higher toward their *"Spiritual Ascension"*) is referred to as *"The Pathway"*—and we call that individual a *"Seeker."*

At the start of *The Pathway*, early *routes* emphasize establishing a strong personal foundation of emotional well-being and mental strength before a *Seeker* is introduced to more advanced exercises and practices.

As a *Seeker* increases their *Awareness* in this lifetime, their spiritual "*Knowingness*" also increases—which is to say their sense of "*certainty*"; a certainty on *Life*, on this and other *Universes*, but more accurately, an increased certainty on *Self* as a practically unlimited "spiritual being" *having* an enforced restrictive "human experience."

One of the goals of "*Systematic Processing*" techniques in *Systemology* is to increase the ability of a *Seeker* to actually control and direct the "*attention*" of *Self* as a "spiritual being"—and as a result, *knowingly* increase command of the "human experience." This is a part of what we mean by "*Actualized Awareness*."

## THREE STATES OF KNOWINGNESS

Raising a *Seeker's* level of *Actualized Awareness* requires, by definition, "bringing what is *hidden* (or not consciously known) up into the realm of *light* or *Knowingness*." We might go as far to say, as an imperfect example, that there are three primary states of *Knowingness*: *actual knowing*, *almost knowing* and *not-knowing*.

*Actual knowing* is what an individual is conscious of and can easily recall as needed. It makes up our "surface" (or "above-the-surface") thoughts; what is *"actually known"* and available to *Self* for "inspection" or analytical thought. This includes what we have *certainty* on as part of our *reality*.

Then, there are other *things* "below-the-

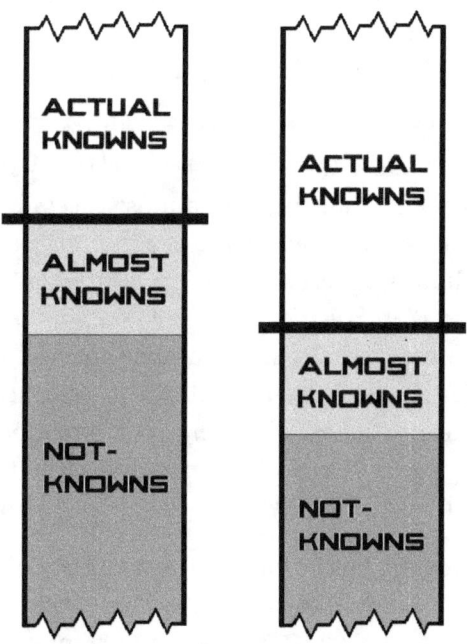

surface" that we do not easily remember (or have any *reality* on)—and these fit our other categories of *almost knowing* and *not-knowing*. The difference between these other two states is how *far* "below-the-surface" a *thing* is.

What you *"almost know"* are those *things* just "below-the-surface"—so *close* to the "surface" that they are almost accessible. This "gray area" includes what an individual is *uncertain* of. With a little assistance (*"Systematic Processing"* techniques), you can actually move a *thing* that is *"almost known"* to an "above-the-surface" state of *"actually knowing"* or remembering again. Only then may it be treated with any *certainty*.

There are also memories very deeply buried "below-the-surface." This includes suppressed data that is not currently accessible—and therefore, presently *"not-known."* Once again, there is a way to move *things* from this state into another state. For this to happen, the previous *"almost known" things* ("just-below-the-surface") need to be "purged" (at least partially) by *"resurfacing"* them into *"actually known" things*.

As more layers of *"almost knowns"* are *resurfaced* into *"actual knowns,"* more of what is *"not-known"* becomes accessible within the "gray area." *Systematic Processing* techniques of *Systemology* are intended to target this "gray area" — promoting increased *realizations* by elevating more knowledge to a state of *Actual Awareness*.

## YOUR FIRST STEPS ON THE PATHWAY

*Systemology* is a "holistic" approach to understanding the human experience. It is not actually a singular "subject" in itself, but rather, a way to "view" the many "subjects" of *Life* and all *Existence*. Its "scope" is not restricted to the rigidly fixed *considerations* of any one "subject" exclusively. Yet, for us to properly communicate its specific intended meaning, *Systemology* does require its own unique basic vocabulary.

The "basic vocabulary" and "*Fundamentals*" of *Systemology* are studied together early on *The Pathway*. They are consistent for the remaining upper-*grades*. It is our *understanding* of them that evolves as we progress.

The entire structure of *Systemology* rests on foundations of earlier material and earlier researches—such as those found in the earlier *grades* of Mardukite Academy. However, in 2019, new developments made it possible for a *Seeker* to start upon *The Pathway* without first spending years navigating around the pitfalls of other avenues and earlier *grade* subjects. As an extension of the original Academy, the Systemology Society continues to map and define the upper-*grade routes* of our philosophy.

The *Fundamentals of Systemology* are explored throughout the *Basic Course.* The critical foundations of its vocabulary and concepts (from *Grade-II*) were concisely collected in 2019 as an essay—*"Mardukite Zuism: A Brief Introduction."* It is summarized below to provide a more complete introduction to the "lessons" of the *Basic Course.* Each "lesson" will go on to examine this data in greater detail.

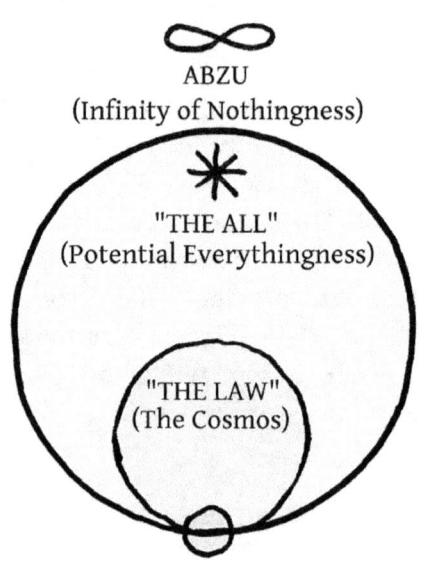

ABZU
(Infinity of Nothingness)

"THE ALL"
(Potential Everythingness)

"THE LAW"
(The Cosmos)

## FOUNDATIONS OF SYSTEMOLOGY

*Mardukite Zuism* is a precursor to *Systemology*. It concerns an intensive archaeological study into the *Arcane Tablets* of Ancient Mesopotamia. Such tablet writings were once used to systematize an understanding of all cosmic knowledge— and they include the Babylonian *Epic of Creation*.

The *Epic of Creation* describes *ALL* ("ANKI") as separated into two *existences*: "AN" and "KI"—literally "heaven" and "earth"—which is to say *"spiritual"* ("AN") and *"physical"* ("KI"). Exterior to, and beyond, the *"potential everythingness"* of all *spiritual* existence and *physical* existence is only an Infinity of Nothingness ("ABZU").

In *Systemology*, we refer to the same two separate states of existence as *"Alpha"*

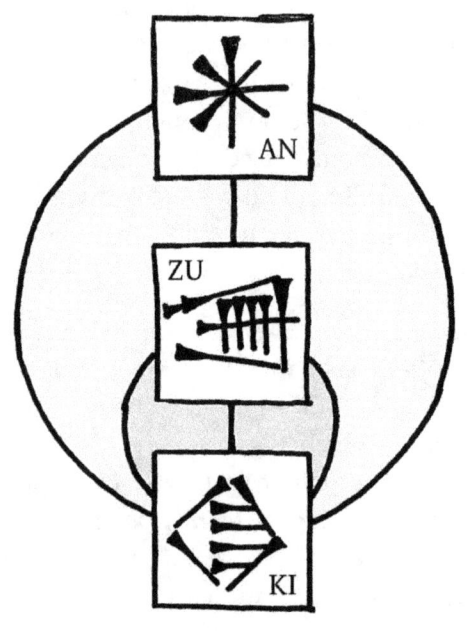

(*spiritual*) and "*Beta*" (*physical*). They are connected only by "*Spiritual Life Awareness*" or "ZU"—a term we have retained in *Systemology* (and for which *Mardukite Zuism* is named). Therefore, we have "*spiritual systems*" and "*physical systems*" connected by "ZU."

The "*Alpha*" *Universe*—of "metaphysical" or "spiritual" energy-matter—is not dependent on the "*Beta*" *Universe* to exist. The two exist independent of one another, except for a single channel or conduit maintaining a connection, which *is* the *Awareness* (the *Spiritual Life-Energy* or "ZU") of an "*Alpha-Spirit.*"

"ZU" originates from an "*Alpha*" (*spiritual*) state, separate and distinct from the conditions of "*Beta*" existence that we experience as the *Physical Universe*. "ZU" is *Awareness*—the *Life-Force* or *Thought-Power* that "acts" or "impinges" on an "organism" in *Beta-Existence.*

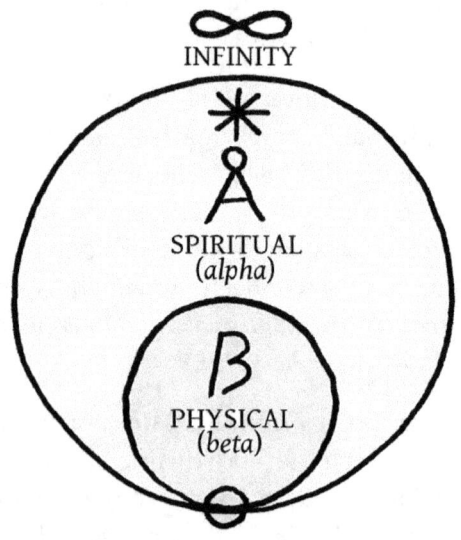

INFINITY

SPIRITUAL
(*alpha*)

PHYSICAL
(*beta*)

For example: the "intention" to read this book, or "commanding" a body to turn a page—those specific components are not actually a part of *this* existence. They are manifestations of a *Spiritual Awareness* (*Alpha*) acting upon an "organic body" (*Beta*). The *"Alpha-Spirit"* is the actual "Eternal" *Self*, which perceives and engages with *Beta-Existence* (*e.g.*, "Life on Earth") by using a "temporary" organic body or *"genetic vehicle."*

The *Alpha-Spirit* engages a *"ZU-Line"*—a *spiritual* "life-line" of *Attention* and *Awareness* ("ZU") energy—to an "organic body" or *genetic-vehicle* in order to directly experience a *"physical"* *Beta-Existence.*

We use the term *"Self-Honesty"* in *Systemology* to describe the original native *"Alpha"* state of true *Self-Directed* "Beingness" and crystal clear *"Knowingness."* *Self-Honesty* is the most basic "personality" or

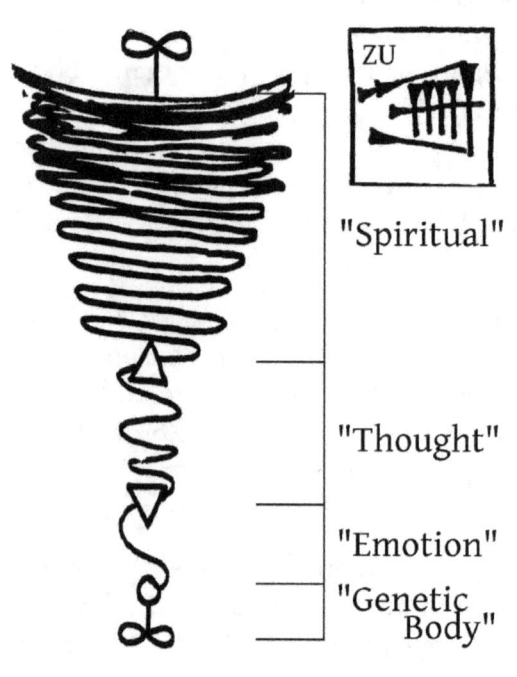

ZU

"Spiritual"

"Thought"

"Emotion"

"Genetic Body"

true expression of *Self* (*Alpha-Spirit*) as "I-AM"—a *Self-Determined* state that is *free* of artificial attachments, automatic reaction-response mechanisms, or enforced (*other-determined*) "*reality-agreements*" concerning the Human Condition.

Applying philosophic routes and systematic methods of *Systemology* in order to return *Awareness* of *Self* to its true "*Source*" is referred to as "*The Pathway.*" Its structure is based on archaic "models" from the "Ancient Near East" (*Mesopotamia, &tc.*) and elsewhere—such as the "*Chakras,*" the Babylonian "*Ladder of Lights*" (*Star-Gates*), and several versions of "*Kabbalah.*"

For example: the Mesopotamians built "stepped-pyramids" as temples—called "*ziggurats*"—serving to remind us of the "ZU" bridging the *spiritual* and *physical* systems. Babylonians constructed *ziggurats* to correspond with *seven* primary "steps" or "*Gates.*"

31

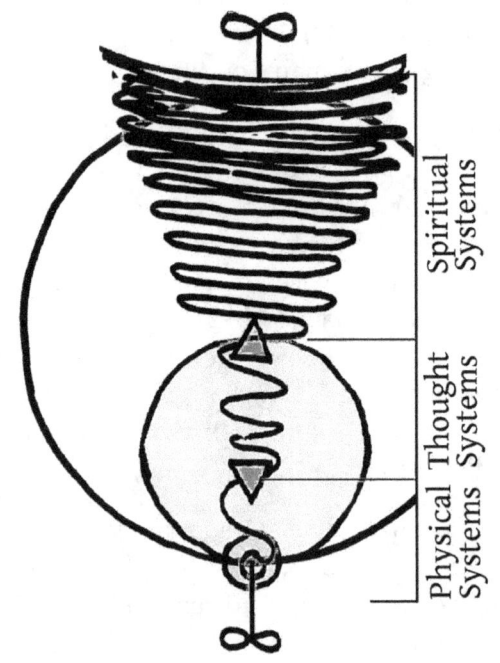

Spiritual Systems

Physical Thought Systems Systems

The "gradients" or "tiers" of the Babylonian *Ladder of Lights* represent *The Pathway*, because they define the *levels* of *Actualized Awareness* (and *Self-Honesty*)—the states of *Self-purification*—between the "standard-issue" *Human Condition* and *Infinity*. This is the *route* we travel for our *"spiritual defragmentation"* or *Ascension*.

# BASIC VOCABULARY REVIEW PUZZLE

## ACROSS

3. The standard-issue default manner of filtering perceptions of the Universe, as Self is experiencing it. (*2 words*)

4. The condition of being misaligned, broken apart, shattered, fractured, distorted, or otherwise separated into parts, compared to its original state.

7. A student or practitioner studying and applying Systemology philosophy.

8. The True Self or I-AM Awareness. (*2 words, hyphenated*)

10. The nature of the Physical Universe or material existence.

11. Another way to say "the agreement about what something is."

DOWN

1. The physical body, or any organic life, may serve as your ___. (*2 words*)

2. Regimen or routine of Systemology practices, techniques or exercises that increase Actualized Awareness of Self.

5. Returning to the original native state (or Source of the Spiritual Self) is known universally as ____.

6. A stream of energy connecting Spiritual Awareness to physical existence. (*2 words, hyphenated*)

9. The progressive journey taken in Systemology is referred to as "*The* ___."

# LESSON FIVE:
# EVOLUTION OF A
# SPIRITUAL SCIENCE

## LESSON FIVE
## EVOLUTION OF A SPIRITUAL SCIENCE

In these *Basic Course* lessons, we are not only concerned with communicating what the "Foundations of Systemology" are, but also in establishing a solid foundation of understanding for the *Seeker* or student that is pursuing these studies. A *Seeker* is not likely to "apply" a philosophy that isn't solidly *"real"* to them.

In *"Lesson 4"* we explored the basic "raw" philosophical data directly derived from ancient *Arcane Tablets*. In this lesson (booklet), we further solidify the foundations of our philosophy by highlighting just a few of the more modern sources of inspiration that led to the evolving development of *Mardukite Systemology*.

This *Basic Course* lesson is a rather incomplete rendering and imperfect tribute. It

*"There is a correspondence between
things seen and unseen;
earth is the shadow of heaven and
humanity is a reflection of divinity."*
—Eliphas Levi

does, however, serve our purposes for introducing a variety of related figures and subjects. It demonstrates that we did not generate the idea of *Systemology* from nothing. But, this is *not* a student's "required reading" list, or even necessarily a "recommended reading" list. It is simply a supportive *bibliography* of sorts—as our work seldom has one.

Our *Systemology* is certainly not based on any *one* of these sources exclusively; nor was *any* one single source taken at "face value" all inclusively during our research phases. And finally, the total culmination of all these points and facets, if simply summed up together, does not equal *Systemology* either. Yet, we did not develop our philosophy in a vacuum; and *Systemology* is a predictable evolution of former understandings.

Unlike other installments of the *Basic Course*, this portion does not include

*"Make use of life, its course is so
soon run;
yet 'systemology' teaches you how
time is won.
I counsel you, dear friend, in sum,
that first you learn
'collegium logicum'.
Then the best of all worth mention —
to 'metaphysics' you must pay
attention,
and see that you profoundly strive to
gain
what is not suited for the human
brain."*

—Goethe, *'Faust'*

"practice exercises" pertaining to its study. As an alternative, a *Seeker* or student is encouraged to personally reflect on the "quotations" cited throughout— and also independently research any aspects of this brief history lesson that may require additional verification for an individual's own intellectual satisfaction.

## JOHN TOLAND 1670 – 1722

John Toland, a notable figure of "freethought" during the *Age of Enlightenment*, is best known for sparking the first modern European "Druid Revival" in 1717. Rather than an emphasis on Celtic mythology, Toland's Druids are "highminded" intellectual philosophers and scientists, not dissimilar from "Freemasons" that officially emerge in England the same year and even met at the same location there: "*The Apple Tree Tavern.*"

*"From the senses arises opinion; and from reason, demonstration. On the former are huddled up the prejudices of the vulgar, following the bare 'exoteric' appearance of things; on the latter are founded the 'esoteric' axioms of the wise, who consider things as they are in themselves."*
—John Toland, *'Clidophorus'*

Toland's work *"History of the Celtic Religion and Learning: An Account of the Druids"* appeared posthumously in 1726, compiled from personal correspondence during his lifetime and prompting *Antiquarian Druidism*. In 2018, the present author published an annotated tercentenery edition of Toland's *"Pantheisticon"* for existing *Systemology Society* members—a short text on natural philosophy and esoteric-philosophy societies.

Key contributions include: a distinction between *"exoteric"* philosophy—what is commonly understood and discussed in public—and *"esoteric"* philosophy, which is communicated privately by a few; and first coining the term *"pantheism"* to describe a philosophy of "divine energy" imbuing all *things*, and a *"Cosmic Law"* that dictates the qualities, patterns or limits for the "energetic interactions" of *things* with each other.

## HELENA P. BLAVATSKY AND
## THE THEOSOPHICAL SOCIETY

Helena Blavatsky (1831–1891), a spiritualist, co-founded the "Theosophical Society" (*New York City*) in 1875, sparking an international movement that widely incorporated Hindu and Buddhist concepts into Western mysticism. Her classic works—*"Isis Unveiled: A Master-Key to the Mysteries of Ancient and Modern Science"* (1877) and *"Secret Doctrine: The Synthesis of Science, Religion and Philosophy"* (1888) —possibly demonstrate the best 19th Century attempts of systematizing "ancient wisdom."

It is perhaps the *Theosophical* movement as a whole—rather than Blavatsky individually—that influenced the present author's early researches into what would eventually develop into *Systemology*. The movement parallels *"New Thought"* in many ways—except that it mostly attracted philosophical-types with mystical ambitions for *Ascension*, rather than targeting professionals seeking luck in business as *New Thought* did. *Theosophy* also reintroduced the disputed scientific concept of *"ether,"* but referred to it as *"Akasha."*

The *Theosophical Society* provided a forum that many creative spiritualists contributed to, including C. W. Leadbeater (1854–1934), Jiddu Krishnamurti (1895–1986), Rudolf Steiner (1861–1925)—and particularly, J. J. van der Leeuw (1893–1934), whose *"Conquest of Illusion"* (1928) is quoted from directly in our text: *"Imaginomicon."*

Key concepts include: modernization of "Eastern" mysticism, the "chakras" and the "cabala"; physical and non-physical systems as interrelated; personal, inter-

*"In phenomenal existence there is nothing that is independent of everything else.*

*Everything is a 'degree' or 'aspect' of whatever Everything is.*

*Our expressions are in terms of Continuity.*

*If all things merge away into one another, or transmute into one another, so that nothing can be defined, they are a oneness, which may be the oneness of one existence.*

*It is not exclusively anywhere where anything is, if ours is one organic existence, in which all things are continuous."*

—Charles Fort, *'Book of the Damned'*

planetary and cosmic evolution; the "Observer-effect" on *Reality*; acknowledgment of an unseen (metaphysical) "council" or "brotherhood" of Ascended Masters that have directly initiated (or communicated with) select individuals on a "path" toward *Ascension.*

---

## EDWIN ABBOT ABBOT
### 1838 – 1926

Written over a century and a half ago by a university headmaster, *"Flatland: A Romance of Many Dimensions"* (1884) remains a timeless relevant classic of philosophy, mathematics, and dimensional-theory. It is a fantasy narrative—comparable to *"Alice in Wonderland"*—told to us by the character 'A. Square' who lives on *Flatland*, a two-dimensional plane inhabited by sentient living 'shapes'.

The "model" that Abbot uses for this fantasy are easily demonstrable to us: the interaction of a *"third-dimension"* with a *"two-dimensional"* plane (or *Flatland*). The "higher" *third-dimension* is not perceived directly by inhabitants restricted to *two-dimensions* of sensory awareness.

*"A. Square"* has an encounter with a sentient unseen "sphere" that is able to speak and interact from the *third-dimension.* The comparison in the narrative rings true regarding limitations of our perception of a "higher" *Universe* or *dimension* while restricted to only perceiving through the human sensory range.

Contribution: *"Flatland"* illustrates inter-dimensional metaphysics quite clearly, introducing an advanced concept to everyday readers in plain language. As such, it ranks fairly high on the present author's "suggested reading" list—particularly for *Seekers* having a difficult time conceiving of a metaphysical *Spiritual* (*"Alpha"*) plane interacting with *Physical* (*"Beta"*) existence. This interaction was once called "unseen perturbation" in *archaic systemology*.

## WILLIAM WALKER ATIKINSON
### 1862 – 1932

Atkinson was a pioneer of the *American "New Thought"* movement. While editor of *"Suggestion"* magazine (later *"New Thought"* and *"Advanced Thought"*) in 1900, he began writing books—leading to the founding of the "Yogi Publication Society" (in *Chicago, IL*)—and then served as president of the *"International New Thought Alliance"* (which still exists today). He eventually wrote over 100 books in 30 years under various names.

By 1920, his publishing company produced dozens of titles for their catalog—

"It is 'you' who lives on forever, not some intangible thing or soul that develops from you at the hour of death.

This 'you' is living in Eternity as much now as it ever will be.

This is Eternity—right now. Many of us, before we grow into an understanding of things, feel that this life is of no consequence—that it is a miserable thing and that true living will not begin until we get out of the body and 'become' a Spirit.

You are a Spirit as much now as ever."

—William Walker Atkinson

with Atkinson using different pseud-
onyms (such as *Yogi Ramacharaka* and
*Theron Q. Dumont*) when writing about
specific traditions. His anonymous works
—*"Secret Doctrines of the Rosicrucians"* (by
*Magus Incognito*) and *"The Kybalion"* (by
*Three Initiates*)—are quite famous and
widely-circulated among "New Age" *esoteric* researchers and practitioners.

Atkinson's "New Thought" was a west-
ernized *American* "answer" to European
occultism, Theosophy and other new
popularly rising interests in "Eastern"
mysticism. It surpassed considerations of
the former "transcendental" movements
—providing the first truly *American* tradi-
tion of *applying* esoteric philosophies.

*"The Law of the New Thought: A Study of
Fundamental Principles & Their Application"* (1902) and the numerous volumes
comprising his library of *"Arcane Teach-
ings,"* proved essential to the founding of

*"We should know what our
    convictions are
        and stand for them.
Upon one's own philosophy,
    conscious or unconscious,
        depends one's ultimate
            interpretation of the facts.
Therefore, it is wise to be as clear as
    possible about one's subjective
        principles.
As the man is; so will be his
    ultimate truth."*

—*Carl G. Jung*

*Systemology* as an "applied philosophy."
In addition to being a source of significant inspiration for the present author
since the 1990's, Atkinson's works are re-
spectfully quoted from several times in
our own *Systemology* literature.

Key concepts include: *Self* operating independent of a body; *Self* as "being soul"
rather than "having a soul"; *Self* having
*one* "spiritual life" but experiencing *many*
forms or "lives"; *Self-Actualization* as a
journey of clearing fragmentation from
many "*consciousness*-levels" for personal
*Ascension*; and that activities of *this* lifetime, either toward increased *realizations*
or toward degradation, carry into experiences of future *lives*.

---

### CHARLES FORT 1874 – 1932

Fort was a self-taught scholar, researcher,
and journalist, residing primarily in New

*"My life is a story of the self-realization of the unconscious. Everything in the unconscious seeks outward manifestation, and the personality too desires to evolve out of its unconscious conditions and to experience itself as a whole. I cannot employ the language of science to trace this process of growth in myself, for I cannot experience myself as a scientific problem."*

—Carl G. Jung

York at the turn of the century. His interest in "curiosities" and "anomalies" of natural phenomenon led to the first and most widely-circulated of his works, "*The Book of the Damned*" (1919).

"*Book of the Damned*" is titled for the idea that such knowledge remains outside the current general understanding, which science generally rejects or ignores, and is therefore "damned" or "excluded." The book pioneered the new field of "anomalistics" and inspired a cult following of "*Fortean*" philosophers. It also includes the first in-depth exploration into UFO-phenomenon (including triangular patterns) decades before common sightings began in the 1940's.

Key concepts: "monistic continuity" (the *ZU-Line* is a "monistic continuum" a "*singularity force*" expressed across an infinite line demonstrating all possible degrees of interaction or manifestation); and

*"Throughout human history, as our species has faced the frightening, terrorizing, fact that we do not know who we are, or where we are going in this ocean of chaos, it has been the authorities — the political, the religious, the educational authorities — who attempted to comfort us by giving us order, rules, regulations; informing — forming in our minds — their view of reality.*

*To think for yourself you must question authority and learn how to put yourself in a state of vulnerable open-mindedness to inform yourself."*

—Timothy Leary

"unseen perturbation" (visible phenomena instigated, triggered, or *"perturbed,"*
by unseen variables or influences).

---

## CARL G. JUNG 1875 – 1961

Carl Jung—originally a serious student of
Freud's *"psychoanalysis"*—is most famous
for developing "analytical psychology." It
is perhaps the best and last attempt to actually understand the "Mind" and "Spirit" of an individual from within the
academic confines of "psychology" as a
medical field.

Jung's work, while clinical, incorporated
mystical themes such as alchemy, Druidism, intuition, past-lives, and even UFOs.
The therapeutic and pop-cultural practice
of analytically "typing" an individual's
*personality*—such as "introversion" and
"extroversion"—is also mostly derived
from *Jungian Psychology.*

*"Human perception involves 'coding' even more than crude 'sensing' — thought is abstraction... Language, mathematics, the schools of art, or any system of human abstraction, gives to our mental constructs the structure, not of the original fact, but the symbol-system into which it is coded."*

—Robert Anton Wilson

As an impressionable youth in the 1990's, Jung's books—and books by those sharing his brand—inspired the present author's interest in pursuing "psychology" (as a means of bridging the understanding between "magic" and "science"). But, after a complete disillusionment with the field at a university level, the author left to independently pursue any related research that might later contribute to establishing *Systemology*.

Key concepts include: existence of universal "archetypes"; potential "synchronicity" of phenomena; confronting the repressed "shadow self"; recognizing social roles and "personas"; measurable biofeedback responses to "words" and "ideas" carrying emotional turbulence; and the idea of an *Individuated Self*, the central "archetype" of an individual, underlying all other artificial or added qualities.

"To operate your brain, you must
  learn how to use your eyes.
'Oh say, can you see?'
  Oh say, can't you see what is
  being done to your eyes?
Who controls your eyeballs, controls
  your mind, imprints your brain.
Oh say, can't you see? — that the
  messages that hit your eyeballs in
  modern television are creating
  realities — imprinting messages
  from the sponsors who are not
  interested in your learning
  how to design your own
  realities."

—Timothy Leary

## FRANZ BARDON 1909 – 1958

Franz Bardon was the most accomplished *"white wizard"* of the 20th Century. His work effectively serves as an alternative to the training and methods of *"black magicians"* gathering in *"dark brotherhoods"* that are more popularly propagated as *New Age "magick"* — such as books and traditions of Aleister Crowley, *&tc.* Bardon's philosophy is probably more comparable to the work of 19th Century magician, Eliphas Levi.

Bardon's proficiency in the "occult" was of such repute that his services were sought personally by Adolf Hitler during the second *World War*. When he refused, Bardon was imprisoned in a concentration camp for nearly four years. Following his fortunate escape, he was arrested in Czechoslovakia for failing to pay taxes

"There is no reality until that reality is perceived.

Our perceptions of reality will, consequently, appear somewhat contradictory, dualistic and paradoxical.

However, the instantaneous experience of the reality of an immediate occurrence will not appear paradoxical at all.

Reality only seems paradoxical when we construct a history of our perception."

—Fred Alan Wolf

on alcohol used for his tinctures. He soon after died of "questionable circumstances" in a prison hospital.

During his brief life, Bardon communicated the most superior "spiritual-magical training program" as *"Initiation Into Hermetics: The Path of the True Adept"* (1956)—a course of personal development rivaling *any* graded curriculum from "magical lodges" and "secret societies" of the *New Age*. It also proved valuable to the present author during experimental research for developing practical applications of our philosophy.

Key concepts include: that each level or *plane* of existence forms a systematic *"matrix"* for the world below it; an application of *electro-magnetism* to metaphysics; incorporation of *"Akasha"* (the *Akashic* principle) into hermetic magic; circulation of energetic systems; and transference of *"consciousness"* remote from the body.

# GENERAL SYSTEMS THEORY
## "SYSTEMATOLOGY"

General Systems Theory, academically known as *"systematology"* (or *"systemology"*), is a "study of systematization— *systems* and their formation" and how they dynamically relate to, or interact with (affect and/or are affected by) other *"systems."* Unlike more "specialized" sciences, *systems theory* is not as concerned with what "type" of *system* is being treated—emphasizing *holism* over *reductionism*.

The idea for "systemology" unarguably began with the systematization of Mesopotamian civilization and cuneiform-language written communications. However, as a distinct field of study—separate from *"natural philosophy"*—it is a relatively new science, emerging publicly in the post-war era of the 1940's and 1950's.

Academically, origins for the field of "General Systems Theory" (GST) are attributed to Austrian biologist Ludwig von Bertalanffy, who proposed that classical laws (such as thermodynamics) might apply to closed systems, but not necessarily to "open systems" (such as living things). The field quickly expanded with the contributions of others, such as "Cybernetics" (Norbert Wiener, 1948) and "Chaos Theory" (1980's).

Key concepts include: communication (feedback loops and exchanges of information between systems); fractal geometry (repetitive patterns); complex and dynamic systems; sealed or closed systems; "open systems"; and "new systems philosophy" (quantum consciousness and the unified akashic field).

*"Right now, you have some sense of being present in your body looking out at the world. But according to physics, this is an illusion of perception. There is no place inside your body where 'you' actually exist. You don't have a particular volume of space or spot that is 'you'. It is an illusion to think that everything outside that volume of space is 'not-you', what you commonly say is 'outside of you'. The best description we can give for this sense of presence is that 'you are everywhere. The main reason that you have more awareness of being in a body is simply because the sensory apparatus of the body commands a great deal of your attention and that much of your attention is linked to your physical senses. We have the illusion that our human bodies are solid, but they are over 99.99% empty space."*

—Fred Alan Wolf

## TIMOTHY LEARY 1920 – 1996

Dr. Timothy Leary served as a psychology professor at Harvard in the early 1960's during some of the first psychedelic research in America. But, by 1962, Leary and other staff involved in the experiments—notably Ralph Metzner and Richard Alpert (later known as *Ram Dass*)—were dismissed from Harvard altogether.

After a rejection from academia, Leary and his associates continued their work independently, sparking the *"1960's New Consciousness"* movement. It's philosophy suggested "dropping out" of participation with the industrialized Western world and returning to "Nature." This also coincided with, and even fed, the early start of the *"New Age"* movement that is still quite prevalent today.

*"Humans believe that they are*
*physical machines*
*that learned to think.*
*Actually they are thoughts*
*that learned*
*to create a physical machine."*
                                    —Deepak Chopra

An intermix of "Eastern thought" is visibly present in the original *New Consciousness* movement. Leary was also undoubtedly inspired by Carl Jung, whom he pays tribute to in his debut book: "*The Psychedelic Experience*" (1964), a manual incorporating meditations based on the "*Tibetan Book of the Dead.*" Its briefer sequel, "*Psychedelic Prayers*" (1966) is primarily a version of the "*Tao Te Ching.*"

Most of the *exoteric* emphasis on Leary's legacy surrounds the use of "psychedelics" directly. However, the "psychedelics" were really a "tool" used by an intelligent and creative psychologist in order to explore, experience, and communicate, about aspects of the Mind that conventional science failed to understand.

It's important to note that effectively applying information earned from these ex-

*"You have changed the past by
no longer letting it influence
actions in the present."*
—Deepak Chopra

periments is not actually dependent on using psychedelics personally. But the theme was certainly a common one among Leary's circle of friends—Allen Ginsberg, Robert Anton Wilson, and Ken Kesey, just to name a few.

Key concepts include: "circuits" of learning; "imprinting" on the Mind; cellular "genetic memory" (the 'electric chain of remembrance'); *Self-determined* control and operation of the Mind; transhumanism; and systematically restructuring ("changing") the Mind as a therapeutic process.

---

## DEEPAK CHOPRA

Deepak Chopra (born in 1946) is one of the few significant influencers of *Systemology* (albeit unknowingly) that is still living at the time of this writing. And again,

*"Live the highest ideal now...*
*You do not have to achieve*
*these states in order*
*to live them now.*
*Living them now*
*is how you achieve them."*
—Deepak Chopra

we see "Westernization of Eastern philosophy and mysticism" as the primary staple defining a modern contribution. Chopra's philosophy is also significantly influenced by Jiddu Krishnamurti (a noted *Theosopher*).

Since 1995, Chopra's *"The Way of the Wizard: Twenty Spiritual Lessons for Creating the Life You Want"* has remained at the very top of the present author's "suggested reading" list for students seeking supplemental outside resources. This book also inspired several popular PBS-TV specials around the time of its release.

Key concepts include: freeing *Self* from the pageantry of playing "roles" in life; *intentions* directing *Awareness*; clearing emotional fragmentation and counter-intuitive thoughts; clearing rigid associations with labels; existence of a "true" or "undefiled" *Self* beneath the artificial attachments and additions.

The present author began compiling material in the 1990's for what is now *Systemology*—but it would take nearly a quarter-of-a-century before it could be adequately communicated. Of course, in the meantime, the world kept turning, as they say. Others were—more actively—also ushering in a new millennium *paradigm*.

In 2004, independent theaters across the country screened a documentary-like film titled: *"What the Bleep Do We Know?"* The film follows a basic modern-day storyline to graphically illustrate some of its points, but it really surrounds various clips taken from interviews with spiritual-minded scientists and physicists.

Fred Alan Wolf is one of the quantum physics professors interviewed, but an important one. His book *"Taking the Quantum Leap: The New Physics for Non-Scientists"* (1982) was the present author's literary introduction to the subject. It is "recommended reading" for those interested in understanding such better. Dean Radin and William Tiller are just a few of the other relevant individuals interviewed for the film.

The internet age has brought with it a whole assortment of *cyber-gurus* and dot-com enlightenment schools. Even the *Mardukite Org* and *Systemology Society* started much in this way on the internet in 2008—and there are more than a few folk (often with greater resources for publicity) that piggy-backed on the example we set. Nonetheless we have pushed through and stood the test of time to be here with you now *fifteen years later!*

There is much talk of using all this information to *"change the world!"* — yes, we

*"After you have reached the higher stages of the journey, you will be glad to discard all of the clothing with which you have covered the Spirit, and finally Self will stand forth on higher planes naked and be not ashamed."*

—William Walker Atkinson

hear that battle call too often to *"change the world!"* We tend to forget that it is us that is *creating* this world; and if anything, it is *us* that requires the "change" and "defragmentation," the "clearing" and "alchemical transformation" of *Self* back into *gold.*

The data on which our *Systemology* is based has "been there all along"—"hidden in plain sight." Much like *General Systems Theory* and *Game Theory* before us, we have simply decided to rearrange the importance and reexamine the significances of available data that might just be useful for broad wide-scope high-view applications. And there is certainly no higher application than the *Great Work,* the journey on a *'Pathway'* that leads to our *Spiritual Ascension*—our return to the *Source.*

*"All that we see or seem
is but a dream within a dream."*
—Edgar Allan Poe

Continue learning
*The Fundamentals of Systemology*
in your next
*Basic Course*
lesson booklet:

**SYSTEMOLOGY PROCESSING:**
**PRACTICES OF SPIRITUAL AWAKENING**

# GLOSSARY

**actualization** : to make actual, not just potential; to bring into full solid Reality; to realize fully in *Awareness* as a "thing."

**agreement (reality)** : unanimity of opinion of what is "thought" to be known; an accepted arrangement of how things are; things we consider as "real" or as an "is" of "reality"; a consensus of what is real as made by standard-issue (common) participants; what an individual contributes to or accepts as "real"; in *Systemology*, a synonym for "*reality*."

**alpha** : the first, primary, basic, superior or beginning of some form; in *Systemology*, referring to the state of existence operating on spiritual archetypes and postulates, will and intention "exterior" to the low-level condensation and solidarity of energy and matter as the 'physical universe'.

**alpha-spirit** : a "spiritual" *Life*-form; the "true" *Self* or I-AM; the *individual*; the spiritual (*alpha*) *Self* that is animating the (*beta*) physical body or "*genetic vehicle*" using a continuous *Lifeline* of spiritual ("*ZU*") energy; an individual spiritual (*alpha*) entity possessing no physical mass or measurable waveform (motion) in the Physical Universe as itself, so it animates the (*beta*) physical body or "*genetic vehicle*" as a catalyst to experience *Self*-determined causality in effect within the *Physical Universe*; a singular unit or point of *Spiritual Awareness* that is *Aware* that it is *Aware*.

**alpha thought** : the highest spiritual *Self-determination* over creation and existence exercised by an Alpha-Spirit; the Alpha range of pure *Creative Ability* based on direct postulates and considerations of *Beingness*; spiritual qualities comparable to "thought" but originating in Alpha-existence (at "6.0") independently superior to a *beta-anchored* Mind-System, although an Alpha-Spirit may use Will ("5.0") to carry the intentions of a postulate or consideration ("6.0") to the Master Control Center ("4.0").

**ascension** : actualized *Awareness* elevated to the point of true "spiritual existence" exterior to *beta existence*. An "Ascended Master" is one who has returned to an incarnation on Earth as an inherently *Enlightened One*, demonstrable in their actions—they have the ability to *Self-direct* the "Spirit" as *Self* and maintain consciousness beyond this existence as a personal identity continuum with the same *Self-directed* control and communication of Will-Intention that is exercised, actualized and developed deliberately during one's present incarnation.

**associative knowledge** : significance or meaning of a facet or aspect assigned to (or considered to have) a direct relationship with another facet; to connect or relate ideas or facets of existence with one another; a reactive-response image, emotion or conception that is suggested by (or directly accompanies) something other than itself; in traditional systems logic, an equivalency of significance or meaning between facets or sets that are grouped together, such as in $(a + b) + c = a + (b + c)$; in NexGen Systemology, erroneous associative knowledge is assignment of the same value to all facets or parts considered as related (even when they are not actually so), such as in $a = a,\ b = a,\ c = a$ and so forth without distinction.

**attention** : active use of *Awareness* toward a specific aspect or thing; the act of "attending" with the presence of *Self*; a direction of focus or concentration of *Awareness* along a particular channel or conduit or toward a particular terminal node or communication termination point; the Self-directed concentration of personal energy as a combination of observation, thought-waves and consideration; focused application of *Self-Directed Awareness*.

**awareness** : the highest sense of-and-as Self in knowing and being as I-AM (the *Alpha-Spirit*); the extent of beingness directed as a POV experienced by Self as knowingness.

**beta (awareness)** : all consciousness activity ("*Awareness*") in the "Physical Universe" (KI) or else *beta-existence*; *Awareness* within the range of the *genetic-body*, including material thoughts, emotional responses and physical motors; personal *Awareness* of physical energy and physical matter moving through physical space and experienced as "time"; the *Awareness* held by *Self* that is restricted to a physical organic *Lifeform* or "*genetic vehicle*" in which it experiences causality in the *Physical Universe*.

**beta (existence)** : all manifestation in the "Physical Universe" (KI); the "Physical" state of existence consisting of vibrations of physical energy and physical matter moving through physical space and experienced as "time"; the conditions of *Awareness* for the *Alpha-spirit* (*Self*) as a physical organic *Lifeform* or "*genetic vehicle*" in which it experiences causality in the *Physical Universe*.

**beta-defragmentation** : toward a state of *Self-Honesty* in regards to handling experience of the "Physical Universe" (*beta-existence*); an applied spiritual philosophy (or technology) of Self-Actualization

**condense (condensation)** : the transition of vapor to liquid; denoting a change in state to a more substantial or solid condition; leading to a more compact or solid form.

**consideration** : careful analytical reflection of all aspects; deliberation; determining the significance of a "thing" in relation to similarity or dissimilarity to other "things"; evaluation of facts and importance of certain facts; thorough examination of all aspects related to, or important for, making a decision; the analysis of consequences and estimation of significance when making decisions.

**continuity** : being a continuous whole; a complete whole or "total round of"; the balance of the equation [ "–120" + "120" = "0" &*tc.*]; an apparent unbroken interconnected coherent whole; also, as applied to Universes in *Systemology*, the lowest base consideration of space-time or commonly shared level of energy-matter apparent in an existence, or else the lowest degree of solidity or condensation whereby all mass that exists is identifiable or communicable with all other mass that exists; represented as "0" on the *Standard Model* for the Physical

Universe (*beta-existence*), a level of existence that is below Human emotion, comparable to the solidity of "rocks" and "walls" and "inert bodies."

**defragmentation** : the *reparation* of wholeness; collecting all dispersed parts to reform an original whole; a process of removing "*fragmentation*" in data or knowledge to provide a clear understanding; applying techniques and processes that promote a *holistic* interconnected *alpha* state, favoring observational *Awareness* of continuity in all spiritual and physical systems; in *Systemology*, a "*Seeker*" achieving an actualized state of basic "*Self-Honest Awareness*" is said to have completed *beta-defragmentation*, whereas *Alpha-defragmentation* is the rehabilitation of the *creative ability*, managing the *Spiritual Timeline* and the POV of *Self* as Alpha-Spirit (I-AM).

**existence** : the *state* or fact of *apparent manifestation*; the resulting combination of the Principles of Manifestation: consciousness, motion and substance; continued *survival*; that which independently exists.

**exterior** : outside of; on the outside; in *Systemology*, we mean specifically the POV of *Self* that is '*outside of*' the *Human Condition*, free of the physical and mental trappings of the Physical

Universe; a metahuman range of consideration; see also '*Zu-Vision*'.

**external** : a force coming from outside; information received from outside sources; in *Systemology*, the objective *'Physical Universe'* existence, or *beta-existence*, that the Physical Body or *genetic vehicle* is essentially *anchored* to for its considerations of locational space-time as a dimension or POV.

**facets** : an aspect, an apparent phase; one of many faces of something; a cut surface on a gem or crystal; in *Systemology*—a single perception or aspect of a memory or "*Imprint*"; any one of many ways in which a memory is recorded; perceptions associated with a painful emotional (sensation) experience and "*imprinted*" onto a metaphoric lens through which to view future similar experiences; other secondary terminals that are associated with a particular terminal, painful event or experience of loss, and which may exhibit the same encoded significance as the activating event.

**fragmentation** : breaking into parts and scattering the pieces; the *fractioning* of wholeness or the *fracture* of a holistic interconnected *alpha* state, favoring observational *Awareness* of perceived connectivity between parts; *discontinuity*; separation of a totality into parts; in *System-*

*ology*, a person outside a state of *Self-Honesty* is said to be *fragmented*.

**genetic-vehicle** : a physical *Life*-form; the physical (*beta*) body that is animated/controlled by the (*Alpha*) *Spirit* using a continuous *Lifeline* (ZU); a physical (*beta*) organic receptacle and catalyst for the (*Alpha*) *Self* to operate "causes" and experience "effects" within the *Physical Universe*.

**gradient** : a degree of partitioned ascent or descent along some scale, elevation or incline; "higher" and "lower" values in relation to one another.

**holistic** : the examination of interconnected systems as encompassing something greater than the *sum* of their "parts."

**imagination** : the ability to create *mental imagery* in one's Personal Universe at will and change or alter it as desired; the ability to create, change and dissolve mental images on command or as an act of will; to create a mental image or have associated imagery displayed (or "conjured") in the mind that may or may not be treated as real (or memory recall) and may or may not accurately duplicate objective reality; to employ *creative abilities* of the Spirit that are independent of reality agreements with beta-existence.

89

**intention** : directed application of Will; to intend (have "in Mind") or signify (give "significance" to) for or toward a particular purpose; in *Systemology* (from the *Standard Model*)—the spiritual activity at WILL (5.0) directed by an *Alpha Spirit* (7.0); the application of WILL as "Cause" from a higher order of Alpha Thought and consideration (6.0).

**interior** : inside of; on the inside; in *Systemology*, we mean specifically the POV of *Self* that is fixed to the *'internal'* Human Condition, including the *Reactive Control Center* (RCC) and Mind-System or *Master Control Center* (MCC); within *beta-existence*.

**internal** : a force coming from inside; information received from inside sources; in *Systemology*, the objective experience of *beta-existence* associated with the Physical Body or *genetic vehicle* and its POV regarding sensation and perception; from inside the body; in the body.

**Human Condition** : a standard default state of Human experience, generally accepted to be the extent of its potential identity (*beingness*).

**imprint** : to strongly impress, stamp, mark (or outline) onto a softer 'impressible' substance; to mark with pressure onto a surface; in *Systemology*, used to indicate permanent Reality impressions marked by frequencies, energies or inter-actions experienced during periods of emotional distress, pain, unconsciousness, loss, enforce-ment, or something antagonistic to physical (personal) survival, all of which are are stored with other reactive response-mechanisms at lower-levels of *Awareness* as opposed to the act-ive memory database and proactive processing center of the Mind; an experiential "memory-set" that may later resurface—be triggered or stimulated artificially—as Reality, of which similar responses will be engaged automatic-ally; holographic-like imagery "stamped" onto consciousness as composed of energetic *facets* tied to the "snap-shot" of an experience.

**knowledge** : clear personal processing of in-formed understanding; information (data) that is actualized as effectively workable understand-ing; a demonstrable understanding on which we may 'set' our *Awareness*—or literally a "know-ledge."

**Master-Control-Center (MCC)** : a perfect computing device to the extent of the informa-tion received from "lower levels" of sensory ex-perience/perception; the proactive communicat-ion system of the "*Mind*"; a relay point of act-ive *Awareness* along the Identity's *ZU-line*, which is responsible for maintaining basic *Self-*

*Honest* clarity of *Knowingness* as a *seat of consciousness* between the *Alpha-Spirit* and the secondary "*Reactive Control Center*" of a *Life-form* in *beta existence*; the Mind-center for an *Alpha-Spirit* to actualize cause in the *beta existence*; the analytical *Self-Determined* Mind-center of an *Alpha-Spirit used* to project *Will* toward the genetic body; the point of contact between *Spiritual Systems* and the *beta existence*; presumably the "*Third Eye*" of a being connected directly to the *I-AM-Self*, which is responsible for *determining* Reality at any time; in *Systemology*, this is plotted at (4.0) on the continuity model of the *ZU-line*.

**mental image** : a subjectively experienced "picture" created and imagined into being by the Alpha-Spirit (or at lower levels, one of its automated mechanisms) that includes all perceptible *facets* of totally immersive scene, which may be forms originated by an individual, or a "facsimile-copy" ("snap-shot") of something seen or encountered; a duplication of wave-forms in one's Personal Universe as a "picture" that mirror an "external" Universe experience, such as an *Imprint*.

**point-of-view (POV)** : a point to view from; an opinion or attitude as expressed from a specific identity-phase; a specific standpoint or vantage-point; a definitive manner of consideration specific to an individual phase or identity; a place or position affording a specific view or vantage; circumstances and programming of an individual that is conducive to a particular response, consideration or belief-set (paradigm); a position (consideration) or place (location) that provides a specific view or perspective (subjective) on experience (of the objective). May also be referred to in our texts as a *"viewpoint."*

**processing, systematic** : the inner-workings or "through-put" result of systems; in *Systemology*, a methodology of applied spiritual technology used toward personal Self-Actualization; methods of selective directed attention, communicated language and associative imagery that targets an increase in personal control of the human condition.

**reactive control center (RCC)** : the secondary (reactive) communication system of the *"Mind"*; a relay point of *Awareness* along the Identity's *ZU-line*, which is responsible for engaging basic motors, biochemical processes and any *programmed automated responses* of a living *beta* organism; the reactive Mind-Center of a living organism relaying communications of *Awareness* between causal experience of *Physical Systems* and the *"Master Control Center"*;

it presumably stores all emotional encoded imprints as fragmentation of *ZU* (within the range of the "*psychological/ emotive systems*" of a being), which it may *react* to as Reality at any time; in *Systemology*, this is plotted at (2.0) on the continuity model of the *ZU-line*.

**reality** : see "*agreement.*"

**Seeker** : an individual on the *Pathway to Self-Honesty*; a practitioner of *Mardukite Systemology* or *Systemology Processing* that is working toward *Spiritual Ascension*.

**Self-actualization** : bringing the full potential of the Human spirit into Reality; expressing full capabilities and creativeness of the *Alpha-Spirit*.

**Self-determinism** : the freedom to act, clear of external control or influence; the personal control of Will to direct intention.

**Self-honesty** : the basic or original *alpha* state of *being* and *knowing*; clear and present total *Awareness* of-and-as *Self*, in its most basic and true proactive expression of itself as *Spirit* or *I-AM*—free of artificial attachments, perceptive filters and other emotionally-reactive or mentally-conditioned programming imposed on the human condition by the systematized physical world; the ability to experience existence without judgment.

**Spheres of Existence (dynamic systems)** : a model of *eight* concentric circles, rings or spheres (each larger than the former) that is overlaid onto the Standard Model of Beta-Existence to demonstrate dynamic systems of existence extending out from a POV of Self (often as a "body") at the *First Sphere*; these are given as a basic eightfold system: *Self, Home/Family, Groups, Humanity, Life on Earth, Physical Universe, Spiritual Universe* and *Infinity-Divinity.*

**Standard Model, The (systemology)** : our existential and cosmological *standard model* or cabbalistic model; a "*monistic continuity model*" demonstrating *total system* interconnectivity "above" and "below" observation of any apparent *parameters*; the original presentation of the *ZU-line*, represented as a singular vertical (*y*-axis) waveform in space across dimensional levels or Universes (*Spheres of Existence*) without charting any specific movement across a dimensional time-graph *x*-axis; The Standard Model of Systemology represents the basic workable synthesis of common denominators in models explored throughout Grade-I and Grade-II material.

**system** : from the Greek, "to set together"; to set or arrange things or data together so as to form an orderly understanding of a "whole."

**thought-form** : apparent *manifestation* or existential *realization* of *Thought-waves* as "solids" even when only apparent in Reality-agreements of the Observer; the treatment of *Thought-waves* as permanent *imprints* obscuring *Self-Honest* clarity of *Awareness* when reinforced by emotional experience as actualized "thought-formed solids" ("*beliefs*") in the Mind; energetic patterns that "surround" the individual.

**ZU** : the ancient Sumerian cuneiform sign for the archaic verb—"*to know*," "*knowingness*" or "*awareness*"; in *Mardukite Zuism and Systemology*, the active energy/matter of the "Spiritual Universe" (AN) experienced as a *Lifeforce* or *consciousness* that imbues living forms extant in the "Physical Universe" (KI); "*Spiritual Life Energy*"; energy demonstrated by the WILL of an actualized *Alpha-Spirit* in the "Spiritual Universe" (AN), which impinges its *Awareness* into the Physical Universe (KI), animating/controlling *Life* for its experience of *beta-existence* along an individual Alpha-Spirit's personal *Identity-continuum*, called a *ZU-line*.

**Zu-Line** : a theoretical construct in *Mardukite Zuism and Systemology* demonstrating *Spiritual Life Energy* (*ZU*) as a personal individual "continuum" of Awareness interacting with all Spheres of Existence on the Standard Model of

Systemology; a spectrum of potential variations and interactions of a monistic continuum or singular *Spiritual Life Energy (ZU)* demonstrated on the Standard Model; an energetic channel of potential POV and "locations" of Beingness, demonstrated in early Systemology materials as an individual Alpha-Spirit's personal *Identity-continuum*, potentially connecting *Awareness (ZU)* of *Self* with "*Infinity*" simultaneous with all points considered in existence; a symbolic demonstration of the "*Life-line*" on which *Awareness (ZU)* extends from the direction of the "Spiritual Universe" (AN) in its true original *alpha state* through an entire possible range of activity resulting in its *beta state* and control of a *genetic-entity* occupying the *Physical Universe (KI)*.

**Zu**-**Vision** : the true and basic (*Alpha*) Point-of-View (perspective, POV) maintained by *Self* as *Alpha-Spirit* outside boundaries or considerations of the *Human Condition* "Mind-Systems" and *exterior* to beta-existence reality agreements with the Physical Universe; a POV of Self *as* "a unit of Spiritual Awareness" that exists independent of a "body" and entrapment in a *Human Condition*; "spirit vision" in its truest sense.

# THE SYSTEMOL

Seekers and students of the *Basic Course* and *Professional Course* will also be interested in the *Advanced Series* of the *Systemology Core*. These volumes are a complete chronological record of the Mardukite New Thought developments from the Systemology Society, published in 2019 through 2023.

The *Systemology Core* begins with the first professional publication released when the *Mardukite Systemology Society* emerged from the underground in 2019, with: *"The Tablets of Destiny Revelation."*

# OGY PATHWAY

The Tablets of Destiny Revelation:
*How Long-Lost Anunnaki Wisdom
Can Change the Fate of Humanity*

Crystal Clear: *Handbook for Seekers*

Metahuman Destinations (*2 volumes*)

Imaginomicon:
*Approaching Gateways to Higher Universes*

Way of the Wizard: *Utilitarian Systemology*

Systemology-180: *Fast-Track to Ascension*

Systemology Backtrack:
*Reclaiming Spiritual Power & Past-Life Memory*

PUBLISHED BY THE **JOSHUA FREE** IMPRINT REPRESENTING

**The Mardukite Academy of Systemology**

THE JOSHUA FREE IMPRINT
JFI PUBLICATIONS

MARDUKITE
ZUISM

**mardukite.com**